BROOKLYN ANTEDILUVIAN

BROOKLYN ANTEDILUVIAN

POEMS

PATRICK ROSAL

A Karen & Michael Braziller Book

PERSEA BOOKS / NEW YORK

Persea Books, Inc.
277 Broadway
New York, NY 1007

Library of Congress Cataloging-in-Publication Data

Names: Rosal, Patrick, 1969–
Title: Brooklyn antediluvian : poems / Patrick Rosal.
Description: First edition. | New York : Persea Books, [2016] |
"A Karen & Michael Braziller book."
Identifiers: LCCN 2015035614 | ISBN 9780892554744 (softcover : acid-free paper)
Classification: LCC PS3618.O774 A6 2016 | DDC 811/.6—dc23
LC record available at http://lccn.loc.gov/2015035614

First edition
Printed in the United States of America
Designed by Rita Lascaro

*This book is dedicated to my father
and to my brothers, Anthony and Mark*

CONTENTS

Despedida: Brooklyn to Philly   1

Typhoon Poem   3

At the Tribunals   5

A Scavenger's Ode to the Turntable
    (Or a Note To Thomas Alva Edison)   7

Brokeheart: Just Like That   9

Uptown Ode That Ends On an Ode to the Machete   11

Ode to the Cee-Lo Players   13

Ode to Not Having Enough Kids to Play a Game of Baseball   15

The Halo Halo Men: An Anthem   16

Violets   21

Lone Star Kundiman (For the Guy Who Seized My Arm
    After I Accidentally Cut the Line for the Toilet in Austin)   22

Wish   25

Kundiman: Hung Justice   27

Fable of the Short Song   29

Instance of an Island   31

The King Won't Kill Me   34

Evidence: Box 1A, Item 1   36

A Field at Night—With Boys   38

Ten Years After My Mom Dies I Dance   40

Children Walk on Chairs to Cross a Flooded Schoolyard   42

Ode to Eating a Pomegranate in Brooklyn   44

Despedida: Quezon City   45

You Cannot Go to the God You Love With Your Two Legs   48

Brooklyn Antediluvian   51

Acknowledgments   67

The wind...

...took us apart with its blue hands, this piece, this piece—
& delivered us to our simultaneous homes.

   —ARACELIS GIRMAY

Forgive my happiness,
I have betrayed you all.

   —ERIC GAMALINDA

Despedida: Brooklyn to Philly

Out here, on the corner of Huntingdon and Trenton,
I can listen a long time to the skaters rail-slide
all June and July at the park, their boards igniting
tight fires against brick and cement, and the fruit lady's
apricots seem to bounce among the topless boxes
crammed into the bed of her pickup truck. This summer,
I said farewell to Brooklyn. I counted each river I crossed.
I know all the bridges by name. I don't owe my madness jack.
The bullhorn on the cab is blasting but it can't drown out
these grim whispers dogging me. In all the worlds I've loved,
I thought I could murder a monster if it had a body to drop,
a set of ribs to measure with a stiff jab and bury my best
left hook. But what about this outcast ache that trails me
like a thick fog of midges, this swarm of spectral pests without
legs or wings. Well, even a beast that can't be seen so easy,
even a creature freaky as Grief has a rhythm to catch. I've learned,
sometimes the only way to lay out a punk who ducks you
is to trick him into singing, a feat you can't achieve
unless you're willing to witness your own dazzling woe,
your maddening clangor. Then you've got to let it all go.
I'll be the first to admit, I've never been beautiful—
except when no one could see me, so beautiful
even I couldn't bear it. That's when I began to imagine
how to float from a silver maple or gather myself
in slow motion like one hundred eighty starlings
then simply burst apart again before the grill of a fast-
moving car. Later, I remembered how good DJs listen
to classic cuts we love on vinyl like a living pulse,
how the tempo's dragged and nudged in the rift
between snare and kick, each meter's kink and quirk,
a chasm that no plain magic can tap and no known math
can predict. The trouble's not a subtle one, to be
without a single nation or a home. And yet, ask

any veteran who has stepped away from his decks
to let them run untouched and he'll tell you: he has heard
the moment when two different tunes left to spin
at the same time line up, sync (sometimes for just
a single measure or less), before those downbeats
buzz loose again and stumble back into the gaps and breaks
of the other track, drifting into their double galaxy
of metal, wood, and space, clattering against one another,
simultaneous grooves, a pandemonium to hone your hearing,
—pickaxe and waxwing, hammer and flutter—the wind-up-
and-jump into the most gladdest double-step romp.
That's what great dancers learn to move to!,
the fickle swing of the meanest demons, the kind of juke
and rock that bears every burden—from cutlass to crib,
Brooklyn to Philly, bamboo to brass. So when the hellion
squads start their ghoulish murmurs, I summon
my every motley bell and nasty drum. I turn it loose.
That kind of thumping will make any ghost hum.

Typhoon Poem

The teacher can't hear the children
over all this monsoon racket,
the zillion spoons whacking
the rusty roofs, the wicked tin streams
flipping full-grown bucks off their hooves.
Everywhere there used to be a river,
there's a bigger river now. Every hard face
on the block is sopping. Even the court
where girls from St. Ignominius ran
the roughneck boys off to play
their own three-on-three in plaid skirts
and church shoes for cash?—forget it.
The whole city's a flash flood
with brawn enough to flush trucks
sideways down the capitol's widest drives:
the crushed tonnage bobs around a bit
at the foot of some Spanish bastard's statue,
before it stalls and pools on white church steps.
Brute pilgrims. Face it, paddling dogs won't
make it, so children got no shot. But quick
thinking, the teacher lashes her students,
two at a time, with wire and stray twine.
She binds them across their breasts
to trees and metal posts lining the street's
half flooded walk. *No goddamned way,*
she swears. She won't let one little one
be washed out, even if their wriggling
makes their armpits bleed.
They'll have to make peace with the vision
of their uncles' and neighbors' blue
bodies bumping past before they fishtail
out of sight. You can't wish away
the deluge. You can't vanish

the bloated carnage-waters. But the tykes
in crew cuts and pigtails, still fastened
to shafts and trunks in ragged rows,
will survive. For now, their teacher
has made them safe by building an orchard
of them in the middle of a city road,
this small chorus of young hard fruit,
this little grove moaning.

At the Tribunals

Once, in a brawl on Orchard I clocked a kid
with a ridgehand so hard I could feel

his top teeth give. His knees buckled
and my homeboy let loose a one-two

to finish the job. I turned around
to block a sucker punch that didn't come.

We ducked under the cops' bright red
hatchets that swung around the corner.

I never saw the first kid drop. He must
have been still falling when I dipped

from the scene and trotted toward
Delancey. He was falling when I stopped

to check my leather for scuff marks.
He was falling when I slipped inside

a dive to hide from a girl who got ghost
for books. He was falling when I kissed

the Santo Niño's white feet and Melanie's
left collarbone and the forehead

of one punk whose nose I busted
for nothing but squaring off with me,

his head snapped back to show his neck's
smooth pelt. Look away long enough

and a boy can fall for weeks—decades—
even as you get down on one knee

to pray the rotting kidneys in your mom's
gut don't turn too quick to stone.

I didn't stick around to watch
my own work. I didn't wait for

a single body to hit the pavement.
In those days, it was always spring

and I was mostly made of knives.
I rolled twenty-two deep, every

one of us lulled by a blade
though few of us knew the steel note

that chimed a full measure if you slid
the edge along a round to make it

keen. I'll tell those stiffs in frocks
to go ahead and count me among

the ones who made nothing good
with his bare hands. I'll confess,

I loved the wreckage: no matter
the country, no matter the machine.

A Scavenger's Ode to the Turntable
(Or a Note to Thomas Alva Edison)

We lifted the precious arm first, then the platter.
    We pulled free the belt, and unscrewed the top.

I didn't take shop or build a whole lot by hand,
    but I was pretty good with a knife. I poked the half-

dull blade clean and gentle through the turntable's
    plastic. I sawed down four inches, straight as I could

make it. Me and my boys—sons of cops, bookkeepers
    and ex-priests—picked up gear other DJs didn't want

no more. One prep-school kid, who just bought
    a shiny new mixer, tossed out his two-month-old

Numark which we picked from the garbage and
    hoisted home. We harvested the slider from the rich

kid's rig. I stripped the wires' tips and soldered them
    to pitch contacts. In a basement of a maple split

in Edison, NJ, we were learning to turn anything
    into anything else, while our mothers played

mah jong in the sala, and our fathers bet
    slow horses and the government bombed Iraq.

We learned to poise pennies on the cartridge head
    so the diamond stylus would sit deep in the vinyl's

groove. A dance floor could turn from winin' to riot
    quick if a record skipped when we spun back

the wax to its cue. We stayed awake from noon
    to noon, digging out from crates some forgotten

voice or violin to scratch. We juggled and chirped.
    We perfected the grind of a downbeat and dropped it

on the bassline coming around. Half trash, half
    hallelujah. Our hands cut Bach to Bambaataa

and made a dance hall jump. We held one ear
    to the syncopated kick and the other to a future

music that no one else could hear. Out of a hunk
    of rescued junk, we built a machine to mix the classics.

We faded and transformed. We chopped up masters
    and made the whole block bounce.

Brokeheart: Just Like That

When the bass drops on Bill Withers'
"Better Off Dead," it's like 7 a.m.
and I confess I'm looking
over my shoulder once or twice
just to make sure no one in Brooklyn
is peeking into my third-floor window
to see me in pajamas I haven't washed
for three weeks before I slide
from sink to stove in one long groove
left foot first then back to the window side
with my chin up and both fists clenched
like two small sacks of stolen nickels
and I can almost hear the silver
hit the floor by the dozens
when I let loose and sway a little back
and just like that I'm a lizard grown
two new good legs on a breeze-
bent limb. I'm a grown-ass man
with a three-day wish and two days to live.
And just like that everyone knows
my heart's broke and no one is home.
Just like that, I'm water.
Just like that, I'm the boat.
Just like that, I'm both things in the whole world
rocking. Sometimes sadness is just
what comes between the dancing. And BAM!,
my mother's dead and, BAM!, my brother's
children are laughing. Just like—I can't
pop up from my knees so quick these days
and no one ever said I could sing but
tell me my body ain't good enough
for this. I'll count the aches right now,
one in each ankle, the sharp spike in my back,

this mud-muscle throbbing in my going bones.
I'm missing the six biggest screws
to hold this blessed mess together. I'm wind-
rattled. The wood's splitting. The hinges are
falling off. When the first bridge ends,
just like that, I'm a flung open door.

Uptown Ode That Ends
On an Ode to the Machete

Me and Willie hail the first yellow
to fly us from Franklin and Fulton
over the bridge to zip up the East Side
where the walls are knocking to Esther Williams
or Lavoe. And Willie daps up Orlando
and I say *What's good!* and it don't take
three minutes for me and Will to jump
on the dance floor or post up at the bar
sipping on Barrilito or to tap on my glass
a corny cáscara with a butterknife
like I'm Tito Puente but I sound more
like a '78 Gremlin dragging its tailpipe
the length of 119th. It's not even five-past-
midnight in El Barrio and I'm nodding
to G-Bo spinning one ill cut after another,
just two degrees shy of the nights' full
swerve, which is to say, at some point,
we stop amid the room's macumba boom
braddah bámbula to watch the dip and sway
of this motley flock and Dear Brother Will
leans over to me and says one word at a time,
"We are all trying to get home."

                    Allow me to translate:
There are neighborhoods in America
whose denizens steady rock their goblins
by the first and last law of moving bodies,
whose best sanctuary, duende and diablo,
rite and act, is the dance floor.
If you haven't been broken by the ocean,
if your own weeping doesn't split you down
into equal weathers: monsoon, say,
and gossip, if you can't stand

at the front door of an ancestral house
with a black saint staring down at you,
if you haven't listened to the town drunks
laughing underneath a tree they planted
so they wouldn't forget your pain,
good chance you didn't inherit the tradition
of summoning disgruntled angels. Armed
with cutlasses, they could teach you
to make anything with that simple blade
or, for that matter, chop anything down.
Bless you and your saddest secrets,
but I once made the pilgrimage to the exact
place where men forge by hand the machetes
of the Philippines, an open-air hut beside
a carabao pasture adorned with magnificent
piles of shit. I'd seen their fine wares split
mahogany and finesse a fat hog's flesh
from its rib. Then I stood beside those open
hearths. I breathed in their fresh stinging steam.
I squatted on the bare dirt floor to pay
proper homage to their sweat and behold
their work from the proper height.
They stoked the embers. They chanted low.
They dropped their mallets in quick
cut time. When I was young, I thought
hard was the mad-dog you could send
across a crowded bar. I thought hard
was how deep you roll or how nasty
the steel you bring. In some
neighborhoods of America, hard
is turning down the fire just enough,
so you could kiss the knife and make it ring.

Ode to the Cee-Lo Players

Any day, give me this nasty static
of street flies, this blunt smoke
ghosting overhead, this brother right here
who slaps half his rent against a brick wall
and won't flinch once though his phone's
blowing up. Right now no orchestra
of jasmine, no honey-hipped
parade could snatch him from this
huddle of petty thieves and shit talkers
trading fire. Sorrow's a kindling too.
This smoldering without wicks
becomes us. If only we didn't burn so fine
standing still, cypher where there's no truth
like a shooter's hot hand gone cold,
where you learn the rules by watching
how stones and cash trade places quick,
and some hustlers are so good
they flip the grins of giddy princes.
Know that I have crouched among boys
whose blistering wit jacks the master
alphabet the canons have handed them.
We have been the young bucks
who bear no standards and rep no set
save the galactic brotherhood
whose initiates have wrung blood
from their own sleeves into public sinks.
Here, on the avenues of chance, no one plays
alone for dollars and rocks. Our anthems
re-draw heaven, hell, and the corner shop.
We have risked more than a clutch
of crumpled singles in our fists.
This is what dice does to us. We kneel
in semicircle. We perfect the slick lean

into the toss. We hone the wrist's flick
and snap our fingers on every sweet trips-run.
Some rules you can't write down. From above,
we must sound like we're speaking in foreign
tongues. Half this game is calling out
our numbers before they even come.

Ode to Not Having Enough
Kids to Play a Game of Baseball

One time, it started with a broomstick and a bag of grapes, us whiffing 'til half the bunch dropped in the mud. Then someone mucking around deep in the brush found an old Rawlings losing its stitches and another boy would rush back to his room to snatch the only bat. We didn't need a full nine-a-side, just one kid to fungo at the plate and one or two others to chase the ball down. You couldn't get plunked in the box like that. No crew-cut knucklehead on the mound with enough of his dad's mean streak to crack you on the chin with some middle-school heat. Mostly, I hit worm burners, but sometimes smacked one deep past shortstop. Every ten shots, we'd take turns and I'd trot back to the dried up, dead grass of left field. Sometimes I had to break back and right, bare-hand side toward the fence, out there, where I learned to read the cut and judge the English.

I was one of three children who shared two gloves. My big brother, Anthony, the lefty who could track fly balls with the wrong paw, and Mark, the youngest, the hustling, husky one with a good gun and nasty knuckle sinker. Each of us eager to race a thing with no legs, to outrun something humming down an imaginary line, two-hundred feet from a collapsing backstop.

In an era of bloody noses and bastard saints, it will always happen that a few restless boys step onto a field and multiply, eighteen bodies in all. And they'll keep at the game until every tree around the puny Church of St. Margaret and Mary goes bare. I know those monsters. They eat splinters. They're filled with kites. Long into October, we give each other busted lips and spit dust when we cuss. Our mother shouts for us down the block, and our father shouts after our mother, and us boys, having heard the terrible crack of wood on hide, up close and far away, learn to scramble in the dark field with so many arms, three dozen useless eyes, all of our hearts beating faster and faster at once.

The Halo Halo Men: An Anthem

We are the halo-halo men

the mix-mix men the fresh-cut-
mango-in-your-mouth men

The men who pee-pee in your Coke
The joke that yokes the beasts

of vinyl and diamond men
The bit-of-salt-to-cut-the-ice men

The wineskins-without-wine
blunt-hilt-of-the-bolo-to-your-head

men We are the how-how men
the carabao men back-to-ten men

Pen-pen men de sarapen
de-kutsilyo men de-alamasen

The when men Come-again men
The middle man and omega men

You build fences for we might
steal your hen men

Kimat and Pang-or men First
to suicide in the cypher men

We use our inside voices
for an outside fight men

say three Hail Mary's
and whisper Hallelujah

flip the new testament
like we do judo men

vodou men raw blood and
garlic men kilawen men

I say ag-yaman ak
you say A-

Violets

A brisk sunset walk home: Lafayette Ave.
After weeks straight of triple layers
and double gloves, the day has inched
enough out of the freeze that I get around
just fine without my hands jammed
in my pockets and my eyes half shut
against the cold. I switchback real quick
and yank a twig jutting out from a trash can
just for kicks. I get going again, swinging the stick
as if I'm conducting this miserable choir
of pigeons at my feet. A good block to go,
I'm about to pick up the pace when I catch
a small flash of dusk out the corner of my eye,
not from the skyline but from the bit of branch
I'm holding—another violet's just sprouted
from my fist, a small flash of welts, a cluster
of indigo, a smack of dark lilac . . . which seems
to happen lately in every season. Matter of fact,
sometimes I look down the street and violets
are spilling out the doors, down the stoops,
into corners and lots. They are pooling at every curb
and mothers hang their heads out the windows
in horror. I carry the violets one by one inside
my apartment. I head straight to my kitchen
and lift the blossom to the light, roots and all,
shaking dirt loose to take a good long look
at these squares of Jesus-purple. I hold it
to my nose, say grace, and clamp my lips down
to pop a petal free. I close my mouth around it,
I pull it onto my tongue to feel its cool silk
and push it against my teeth. I chew
and chew some more and I say *why not*,
for we live in the ongoing American epoch

in which a man can shoot a child in the eye
or back and not be convicted of murder.
Who's got what magic now? Most days I am one
of the hundred million who just watches
the violets multiply. Then some nights,
I sit in my kitchen eating this one perfect flower.
Stupid, I know. But I've held things in my mouth
with more sugar and felt less blessed.
If you want to know, this violet tastes
of the slightly rotten whiff of a late April rain,
the muddy musk of old piano keys,
a dusty box emptied of nickel casings
and old colognes. It tastes a lot like
the small twitch of fog my breath makes
against my lover's belly. This flower
in case you've forgotten has sprouted
from my own fingers, maybe even deeper—
my liver, my spleen. Turns out,
rage is a flower like this one, like
that one, like this. My body's
the right mulch for it. Sometimes
a man is only as lucky as his hands.

Lone Star Kundiman (For the Guy Who Seized My Arm After I Accidentally Cut the Line for the Toilet in Austin)

I keep saying it was the way you took my arm,
the small imperceptible squeeze, that tiny shove,
the way you told me *Get to the back of the line*,
how you eyed me to my place with your little smirk.
Some keep saying it was the rum. I keep saying
it was history. Truth is, I could have done much more
than smack you a couple times across your right eye.
Truth is, I couldn't stop to consider how we both live
in a country mostly afraid of the difference between
strength and power. Three times I warned you not
to grab me like that again. You did it anyway.
I'm long familiar with both the master's sinister hand
and mine, and I, unlucky, couldn't bring myself to wish
a single kind thing for my puny heart. Just like
the pop songs preach: *If I had to do it all again,
I wouldn't change a thing*. I promised no more
heart songs, but some want to hear what a heathen
prays for when he bows his head and drops his fists.
In Texas, you can sit in a diner packed with white folks
who dip their sweet potato fries in honey Dijon, while
you practice what it's like to be the last man on earth
or the first one to land in a city where no one sees you.
You can pray for an ordinary night, a stroll down
a side-street off West 5th where locals nod and say
Good Evening. You can head to the john with your bladder
throbbing like a jellyfish and trust the gentle manners
of the South. Well, after I was ushered out, I walked
the half-mile with a friend from Tap Lounge to El Camino
laughing at the way you touched your own soft hand
to your soft cheek, jaw-dropped, for though I was the one
kicked out of the bar, you would most likely grab
another brother not so easily again. I guess whoever
taught me and you about love—they taught us wrong.

My hand's quick trip from my hip to your chin, across
your face, is not the first free lesson I've given. And
you're not the first knucklehead I've had to instruct
in the company of strangers with an open-hand left cross
delivered like a love song. Consider it a public
education. No white boy left behind.

Wish

If the engineers manage to crunch another
hundred billion digits in their niftiest chipset yet
and craft their swiftest killing missile to date
then congratulate each other with the tiny chimes
of their slender perfect flutes, if they are paid well
and sleep well for the coming schedules of doom
and the designs down to the very joule
are symmetric and beautiful, the way hills
in the distance are sometimes symmetric
and beautiful—split down the crestline
(from birdseye)—and the laser sights' path
sweeping along them reminds us of a spine's
precision too, if the same hills are walloped
by carpet bombs, so the goats kicking their way
up the hillside are roasted by the explosion, if this
still goes on as it often does with schoolchildren
with their hands on their ears and their heads
between their knees or one hand on a rope
leading a billy goat to a patch of grass
as the rockets streaks down to make war
a kind of weather, if this triple sorrow like points
of a tyrant's compass, if this battlemind, if this
Fuckyou I'm dreaming of figs, if this crate pushed
out the back of a truck or dropped from low-flying
planes or copters, if the children of my brother,
nonetheless, have their way with singing
and their singing means no one asks them
to pledge allegiance to fires by plucking
the fires' embers from their tongues, if this war,
I mean, this one that follows the one before it, persists,

let me not be the last to scoop
two small children, blindsided, into my arms

and feel their awkward bodies squirming
to be free, one sticking a desperate pinky up my nose
to make some space for his escape, the other, flipped
upside down, kicking me in the chin, let me know
their hip bones through their polar bear pajamas
in summer and their little teeth cracking me
on the side of the head breaking a bit of skin
above my ear as they cackle away tickled
by their unshaven lunatic uncle weeping
with joy when he finally sets them
loose on to the hardwood floor where
they tumble and wriggle like a couple ugly fish
until they grow human legs and scramble
to their brand new feet and scoot to the room
where there is a piano for them to bang on
where they can make an afternoon music
to piss their pops off mid-nap—where
they may craft the kind of nonsense
to teach kings what wicked screaming
—hoot and demonhowl and caterwaul—
two big-lunged munchkins can even make
with just their little mouths
like the sound of jet engines
winding their last time down.

Kundiman: Hung Justice

Love, a child dreamt hard of
bread and got history

instead. Someone dreamt of
maggot-jewels in meat and

brought out blades in the name
of good science, ardor.

But who'll list kinships in
English between slaughter

and laughter? Who'll recruit
heaven's splendid refuse,

junk, our silent brigades
of busted blue-black horns,

swordless squadrons, the hum
and ruckus of strung-up

ghosts, the delirium
of angels and muddy

hilt and rust, this finch-quick
trigger, dull dagger third-

muscle deep, gas-sopped rag?
Who's got lungs for song? Hoist

not a schoolyard's one taut
noose or red bunting bloom.

My America, you
can't even love a face

as handsome as a bomb.

Fable of the Short Song

Once there was a girl who threw five bricks into the sea. The bricks came up birds. They flew near God's head. They skimmed his right ear. Each brick-turned-bird whispered its own name, and to each bird God said, *Rain then*.

And wasn't it God who walked out to the shallows and snatched back the five birds' names? He sent each bird in the five principal directions of a compass.

The birds had nothing left to say.

This made all the fish in the sea so sad, they threw their bodies up onto the shores, where they could feel the sun full on their flapping bodies until they fell still and their carcasses baked dry and bare.

The girl who first hurled the bricks that became the birds took a walk along the breakers. She came upon this open graveyard on the sand, its multitude of skeletons, the fishes' thorny ribs.

She collected the best of the bones. She began to see the way they fit curve to curve and tip to exact tip. She began to piece them together, healing one jagged edge to another. She left some fractures and fissures just so, places for the light to hide or shine through when she held them up even to the slimmest moon.

Out of those thousands of bones, she had made a single humongous one. She kept walking through the graveyard of the plenty dead—with the gigantic femur hoisted on her shoulder. She gathered bones and sewed together a spine, a tail, too, four legs and the long sad lines of a head.

Exhausted, she went to sleep at last under a tree and left that trellis of a body standing at the edge of the sea.

Since God didn't know the word for flock of swallows, a typhoon came instead. The hillside clay turned to mud. It took weeks for the rivers to retreat. The girl woke. She carried armloads of the new-made muck and draped the fishbone cage with thick sheets of clay. She piled mud upon mud, slapping muscle into it, a thick neck, a bulky rump. She pressed her tongue once on each side, high on the skull. She stroked ears into points. She coaxed a mane to fall about its neck, pulling each strand carefully as if guiding drops of rain down the soft length of vines or rousing tears from orchids with her fingers.

That's when God knew nothing could be beautiful only standing still. So he took the whip his father used to beat him with and snapped the mud and fishbone steed on its big ass. The mudhorse galloped through the breakers, past a cove of bats and lizards, the sound of crushed calcium fading under its hooves.

Once the beast was gone, God took a last handful of chalky fish remains, pounded them with a pestle until they could fit into very small mouths. He flung the bony bits far enough for the nameless birds to catch a whiff of the God that shooed them away in the first place. The birds did come back, but it was the girl who received them. They landed on her wrists, elbow and head.

There was one tune the girl could sing well. It was exactly four notes long. She planted one syllable from that tune in each of the birds' throats. She made a fifth syllable up. She blew the tune into their little mouths. She sent them off again to be lost in the principal directions. She waited a little while for the horse to finally return. With both hands, she took hold of its beautiful ears. She climbed into its maw headfirst. And once she was all the way in, she told the horse to go.

Instance of an Island

One way to erase an island is to invent
a second island absolved of all the sounds
the first one ever made. We don't know
who concocted this one, where the triggerfish
and clowns fade to inky neon dashes under
a fisherman's skiff. A few plastic pontoons
knock around makeshift slips. Dusk coaxes
from the shore the small, dull chime
of a spoon against a pot and TV voices
flash slow across a cliff. Two pink lovers
in matching swimwear kiss their glasses
at the edge of a blue pool built just low enough
into the hill so the couple can gaze into the sea
and think of infinity. Many, many years ago,
a great emperor wiggled his finger
and commanded his army to corral all the lepers
in his domain then pack them into a sailing ship
to be delivered to the missions on this cluster
of verdant volcanic rock. The emperor's orders
to his captain were clear: if the monks refused
the ship's freight, the skipper was to simply
dump the whole sick cargo far from any shore.
Other incurables followed in lots over time,
or trickled in, hiding from nearby tribes,
or banished from other lands to live among these
lush slopes of mahogany, papaya, and weeds.
Two women, Filomena and Josefa, arrived
within days of one another. By then, each had lost
most their toes, though they had ten
full fingers between them, each woman
with one hand still intact. No one is sure
how it began, but once a week the pair
would knock on the door of the scowling

Madre Clementina to borrow the hospital's
only guitar, carved from jackfruit and cracked
pretty bad along the back. To these women—
no big deal, for Filomena once transcribed
the early moonlight serenades of the horny friars
in the Royal South for the brats of an Andalusian
duke. Josefa was the daughter of a carpenter,
a maker of tables to be exact. She learned
to play a harana's tremulous melodies
on her mother's banduria at the age of three.
The pair of outcasts would stifle laughs, thrilled
to earn the crusty nun's grudging *Yes*, then
amble out to lowtide and find a flat rock to share,
so they could prop the old guitar on both
their laps, the one bad wrist of each woman
unwrapped to their stumps, pulled for now
behind their backs as they looked past the bay
toward the violent waters that first carried them
here—and they jammed. Filomena with the five
deft hammers of her left and Josefa with her right,
thick-muscled—both blue-veined and furious,
scrubbing from the instrument all those wicked
rhythms from Castile to Nowhere, on a fragile
scrap of furniture that could barely hold its tune.
They sat shoulder to shoulder and thigh to thigh,
their good hands brushing from time to time.
What they couldn't remember, they made up,
and everything they made up disappeared
past the lagoon and over the ocean, every note
in every run, every lie and desire, every nick
and crack in the jackfruit, the fat harmonics
plucked from the old nun's grunts, six taut strands
of gut whose chords skimmed the water

like night locusts in bursts of low clouds
and which bore everything in front of them and behind,
the brine of the women's necks mixed with the salt
of the lagoon, the cliffs, the spoons, the bright
nimbus of the West dipping like a noose,
the future of pontoons and fake tits, the history
of nifty crowns pried loose of their jewels,
the jiggle of a little finger gone still.

One way to erase an island is to invent the waters
that surround it. You can name the waters
which will turn all the sounds the island makes into salt.
It will teach you to listen to everything you love
disappear . . . or you can invent a song so big
it will hold the entire ocean.
                             Josefa and Filomena
rocked in the dark, hip to hip, joined by that third
body of wood, which made sure there was
nothing left in the unbroken world
to possibly make them whole.

The King Won't Kill Me

today. He's cleared the court, torn up
the last treaty, trounced the villages
bordering the empire's southernmost
state, rounded up their dark denizens
and given the hundred skinniest to split
among his governors. I wore shackles
once on a boat across the largest ocean
in the universe, but I was the last among
my captive people to forget how to laugh
and the first to remember our tribal names.
In that time, I learned the whipman's slang,
for when the noble children came to gawk,
I'd listen to them, mimic, until I could
speak back, ask questions, chat them up
for fairy tales, prayers, ridicule, and lies.
Dumb luck, one runt traded me a book
for my right thumb through the bars
of my cage. In no time, I learned to read
all the secrets of their God. Then,
Minor Governor caught me making
a small group of children dance
to my crafted blasphemies, damning us all.
He had me dragged before the King.
His Majesty asked me why I believed
I'd been brought before him, so I called to mind
a passage I memorized from their holy book
about a pale man's rib and sang it in the melody
with which my mother used to bid farewell
to summer every year. The King sneered first,
then held his big belly and laughed. *Take him
away. Take him—away.* I thought, for sure,
it was my death, but it's been 11 years
and the King no longer goes to church

on Sundays, he beckons me to court instead
to make him laugh and sometimes weep.
He calls me *Nearer, my pumpkin, nearer*
then caresses my cheek. Some afternoons
I'm cuddled so close to him I'm sure I could
slip from his fat knuckle one of his big bright
ruby rings. He kisses me from my right elbow
down to each of my four fingers' tips. I tell him
how his darling left hand is so chubby sweet
and I vow, one day, to take the whole
goddamned thing in his sleep.

Evidence: Box 1A, Item 1

To those who plead *Not guilty* I say: a poem
is a field. Exhibit #1: I haven't said a thing
about my hand in murder. I repeat: a poem
is a field. And inside this particular field a man
yells "Hee!" to urge a bull toward the border
between the unpaved earth and the road.
When the bull reaches the end of the field,
the animal turns. The man, my uncle, gets up
early to start the work and finish by noon
then polish off a bottle of rum at a card game
with his boys. But first, at some point, the bull
will get tired and my uncle will hitch a second
bull to the plow. The poem is a field. What enters
the field enters the poem—the man, my uncle,
his several beasts, the plow. But then a boy,
my cousin, comes running to tell my uncle
a man is dead. The bull stops working. A man,
a bull, a boy are standing in the middle of a field
and what's entered is the news of a murder.
The boy won't bring the name of the shooter
though he knows who he is and who paid him.
The man, my uncle, looks out at the hills then
at the boy who brought the news and who is
weeping now. If I think I'm not guilty then
how come you still don't know where I stand.
The ditch is in the field. So is the road. My uncle
yokes a third bull and moves on. In lecture halls,
I was taught I can make a field appear. I was told
to erase myself from the field. And then, just
outside my family's smoky village, I entered
a real field with hip-high cogon grass. I followed
my uncle and cousin who slashed a path. I carried
a real bucket and a real blade and three children

hurried behind me. They called this field holy
because it belongs both to the newly murdered
and the decades-long dead. If you've chosen
to erase yourself from slate, I already know
where you stand. I was taught to sweep the crypts
of our beloveds then kneel at their stones to rinse
their death dates with fresh water and scrape
with a knife the contours of each letter etched
in granite until our family's name came clean.

A Field at Night—With Boys

Balacad, Ilocos Norte, 1985. Late at night, the men of this village have
led twelve boys to a newly-plowed field. Most everyone else is sleeping.
There's hardly a moon to light the clearing. The men make random
pairs of the groggy boys: the scrawny and the badass, the beast and the
pipsqueak. Everyone will fight everyone.

One of the elders yells, "Hee!" and the young ones grab each other blind
by the scruff. They punch each other in the ear and ribs. They tussle and
grunt and roll in the upturned dirt and dung. They smell terrific as pigs.
They try to snap their opponent's forearm or dislocate his elbow. At no
point does anyone call anyone's name in the dark, let alone his own. They
don't cry out or even talk. If they wince at all, they do in silence. The
blackness makes them familiar. James knows his manong Oka's deltoid.
Junar recognizes his baby cousin's deltoid and Mario's cheekbone by touch
alone. They reek of the afternoon's cigarettes and grilled fish.

It will be hours before they finally leave the field, some half-staggering,
dragging their limbs like drenched rags. The water from the well will
be good, cold. Two older men will take turns hauling a huge bucket up
through the deep cinder block shaft. The boys will huddle for their turn.
Then, one by one, each will plunge his wrists, scooping into his cupped
palms more water than his mouth can possibly hold, careful not to muck
the well. In the near absence of light it will look as though this one is
lifting blue milk to his lips. The water will twine through his slender fin-
gers. He will sip so deeply and so long, he could be praying. He could be
peering into the small wreckage of a twisted harp or weeping into a tiny
shimmering net. He could be using his teeth to free his hands, untangling
its silver filaments. Or it could be a mask. And he's peeling all the long
threads of steel clinging to his eyes.

For now, two of the older men are walking through the writhing piles,
surveying each thick violent braid—more by sound than sight. The boys
almost don't know when to stop. They pin one another to the fresh wet

earth. They tap their hands in quick triplets when they are about to be maimed, so they do halt for a bit, but under watch, they get snarling again right away. When an elder shouts "Op!", the boys switch up partners for the next round of scuffling. And when the older men finally separate the young ones for the night, no one is congratulated. No one is coddled. They are exhausted and thirsty. The boys can barely rise from their knees.

Ten Years After My Mom Dies I Dance

The second time I learned I could take the pain
my six-year-old niece, with five cavities
humming in her teeth, lead me by the finger
to the foyer and told her dad to turn up
the Pretenders—"Tattooed Love Boys"—
so she could shimmy with me to the same jam
eleven times in a row in her princess pajamas.
When she's old enough, I'll tell her how
I bargained once with God because all I knew
of grief was to lean deep into the gas pedal
to speed down a side road not a quarter-mile
after scouring my gut and fogging my retinas
with half a bottle of cheap scotch. To those
dumb enough to take the odds against Time,
the infinite always says *You lose.* If you're lucky,
Time grants you a second chance, as I was lucky
when I got to hold the hand of my mother,
how I got to kiss that hand before I sprawled out
on the tiles of the hallway in the North Ward
so that the nurses had to step over me while
I wept. Then again, I have lived long enough
to turn on all the lights in someone else's kitchen
and move my hips in lovers' time to the same
shameless Amen sung throughout the church
our bodies build in sway. Oh magic, we move
through the universe at six hundred seventy million
miles per hour even when we are lying absolutely still.
In Brooklyn, a man can prove he's a sucker for ruin
by dropping an old school toprock on the G platform
at Metropolitan despite the fifty-some strangers
all around him on the platform. Sure, I set it off
in my zipped up three-quarter coat when that big girl
opened the thunder in her lungs and let out her badass

banjo version of the Jackson 5, all of which is to say,
thank you for the kind of wacky anguish that leads me
to a sticky floor like this late-night lounge under
a century-and-a-half-old bridge where I'm about to twirl
a mostly deaf woman by the hand and listen to her whisper
a melody she's making up to a rhythm she says she feels
only through her chest, how we will hold each other
until the lights come up as if two strangers
couldn't dance this long to the same sorrows
and one body couldn't sing two songs.

Children Walk on Chairs
to Cross a Flooded Schoolyard
—Taytay, Rizal Province, Philippines

(based on the photo by Noel Celis)

Hardly anything holds the children up, each poised
mid-air, barely the ball of one small foot
kissing the chair's wood, so
they don't just step across, but pause
above the water. I look at that cotton mangle
of a sky, post-typhoon, and presume
it's holding something back. In this country,
it's the season of greedy gods
and the several hundred cathedrals
worth of water they spill onto little tropic villages
like this one, where a girl is likely to know
the name of the man who built
every chair in her school by hand,
six of which are now arranged
into a makeshift bridge so that she and her mates
can cross their flooded schoolyard.
Boys in royal blue shorts and red rain boots,
the girls brown and bare-toed
in starch white shirts and pleated skirts.
They hover like bells that can choose
to withhold their one clear, true
bronze note, until all this nonsense
of wind and drizzle dies down.
One boy even reaches forward
into the dark sudden pool below
toward someone we can't see, and
at the same time, without looking, seems
to offer the tips of his fingers back to the smaller girl
behind him. I want the children
ferried quickly across so they can get back
to slapping one another on the neck

and cheating each other at checkers.
I've said time and time again I don't believe
in mystery, and then I'm reminded what it's like
to be in America, to kneel beside
a six-year-old, to slide my left hand
beneath his back and my right under his knees,
and then carry him up a long flight of stairs
to his bed. I can feel the fine bones,
the little ridges of the spine
with my palm, the tiny smooth stone
of the elbow. I remember I've lifted
a sleeping body so slight I thought
the whole catastrophic world could fall away.
I forget how disaster works, how it can turn
a child back into glistening butterfish
or finches. And then they'll just do
what they do, which is teach the rest of us
how to move with such natural gravity.
Look at these two girls, center frame,
who hold out their arms
as if they're finally remembering
they were made for other altitudes.
I love them for the peculiar joy
of returning to earth. Not an ounce
of impatience. This simple thrill
of touching ground.

Ode to Eating a Pomegranate in Brooklyn

When I fall in love again I will have another heart
and a second set of eyes which is one way

to watch the woman you love   grow old

The story of my heartbreak started like this:
someone gave me a key that opens many doors

I traded it for a key that opens only one
I traded that one for another and that for another

until there were no more doors
        and I had a fist full of keys

At any given moment only part of the world is gruesome

There are three pomegranates in the fridge
waiting to be broken open

When I fall in love again
my beloved and I will spit seeds into the street

until the birds come to pluck them

When I fall in love I'll count the tick
of little pits in city puddles

I'll forget the dead
        and count the doors instead

Despedida: Quezon City

My gentle, drunken friends, my four bags,
    strained to the teeth, are now packed.
Check out how well I know your city

by my goodbyes . . . To Grotto Mary with bird-
    shit brow, to boys of half-court flip-flop runs,
to checker game hustlers of Sikatuna,

to the single, slender ankle dangled
    from the jeepney, to the skeltered treble
of KTV saloons, farewell. To this family

asleep in barrows, farewell. To power brokers
    yanking lines, to the pauper with a fist
full of jasmine, to the hammer traveled

a thousand miles, to North Ave. bangups,
    Quiapo ripoffs, and City Hall breakdowns.
To a taxi's backseat musk, you gave me

the smell of the sea come rushing a metropolis,
    the smell of an ocean come to soak our children
to their bones, to skunky scotch, to Rock,

Jimmy, and Krip, to the makeshift shops
    and tattered plastic signs, to tenth-floor
bureaucrats. How many afternoons

I put ice to my earlobes as a way
    to stay the wicked heat. To the counterfeits
of winter, farewell. What have I learned?

Sometimes this city goes dark for no
    apparent reason and you can know
the burnt hue of a stranger's skin

by candlelight. And when the electricity
    comes back you need nothing but nod
to one another as your only despedida.

Goodbye to the rot-toothed girl with bad math,
    clutching a plastic sack of coins—my bags, little one,
are packed. To the EDSA skylines pried open

at 3am, to the illusion of falling giants,
    to the felling of giants for real, to Jiggs
and Banjo, to you blue nag of a nun,

to all cabbie scams, gun in the front box,
    loaded, goodbye, for now
                                —goodbye.

And to the beer guzzlers of Xavierville
    who dream in ska, my dreadful philosophers,
my punk rock sweethearts, please don't laugh

from the other half of the world if in a year
    I'm still summoning you into the rooms
of Brooklyn, among dear poets there,

one by one, and my loved ones of that island
    will know you—who are loved ones
of this island—and we'll fling rum to the floor

from our fingertips asking the god of cane
    to bless us all with long life, sweet breath,
and the demons' blasé drums gone funky.

When calculus fails,
    after all: poems.

I used to think you had to rise into the air
    some 30,00 feet to behold the sum
of a city's light all at once. All I did

was step outside into the goblin dark
    and see the bodies for myself.
Some might say we are bound

together because, every generation,
    a monster with one or a million
eyes seems to come to try like hell

and take away our tongues.
    But it's just us figuring out how to live
on what the floods entrust to us.

Case in point: I recognize the many ways
    to say *Good riddance* in every city
and yard I've been. And I've had to learn

entire languages without ever actually
    speaking. It's another consequence of love.
Everything I say is half broken

before it even leaves my mouth.

You Cannot Go to the God
You Love With Your Two Legs

And because you're not an antelope or a dog
you think you can't drop your other two limbs down
and charge toward the Eternal Heart.
But you must fall in love so deeply, those other legs
are yours too, the ones that have hauled their strange body
through a city of millions in less than a day
at its own pace, in its own pain,
and because you cannot make the pace of the one whom you love
your own and because you cannot make the pain of the one you love
your own pain, your separate aches must meet somewhere
poised in the heaven between your bodies
the skylines turned on their sides
reminders of what once was, what every man and woman
must build upon, build from, the body, the miserable,
weeping body, the deep bony awkwardness of love
in the bed. If you've kissed bricks in secret
or fallen asleep where there was no bed or spent time
lighting a fire, then you know the beginning of love
and maybe you know the end of it and maybe you know
the far ends, the doors, where loved ones enter
to check on you. It's not someone else speaking
when you hear I love you. It's only the nighttime
pouring into the breast's day. Sunset, love. The thousand
exits. The thousand ways to know your elbow
from your ass. A simple dozen troubled hunters
laying all their guns down, that one day
they may be among the first to step
into your devastated rooms
and say *Enough now, enough.*

Brooklyn Antediluvian

The kid, no more than thirteen, backpack
slung over the shoulder, flanked by two

girls probably from his same grade
in white button-down shirts and school-

gray skirts. They walk so light, reeds ought
to be splitting this late-March breeze

so their fine stride's got the right soundtrack.
Young dude looks me up and down

in my doorway. It's about three o'clock
on Tuesday, Montrose Ave., a half-block

from the L, when most the middle school crews
come rising about five at a time from the subway.

He doesn't break his gait to point
at my I-heart-Brooklyn sweatshirt and say,

It don't fit. I think he means I'm too fat
for the pullover, but he says *Nah. It don't fit.*

He's not locked on my eyes for more
than a second, walking past me on Montrose—

the name of an Avenue whose two Roman
syllables imply hills and slopes banked

from foot to crest in roses and I try to conjure
not just this street but the whole borough

from East River to Kosciuszko souped-up
for miles with those prickled vines and lobes

and lobes of red. My name, in Spanish, means
rosebush. In Scotland, there's a field called Rosal—

a village sacked and looted by English dukes
so their sheep could graze on bloody grass, get fat,

then surrender their wool, hide, gristle,
and bone in anonymous service to the throne.

There are no roses there either. In Old Norse,
my name means field of horses. And maybe

there was a time those beasts galloped down
the Scottish hillocks every other day in spring,

and maybe a steaming new foal from a mare's
huffing body staggered, still sopping, into the herd.

This young brother right here swings the knot-
end of his tie from his left fist. Could be, next fall,

his good shoulders will square and the first
thin line of fuzz will etch the strong angles

of his jaw. I want to ask him, *What's your name?*
Maybe he already knows my name means

nothing. Even in a town whose backroads I know
so well I could still slip a cop tailing me twice

in one night, a town whose wooded dirt paths
beside the Northeast Corridor are narrow enough

to kiss a white girl hard and for her to bite
my skinny clavicle clean through my secondhand shirt

and for the world of New Jersey to forget that kiss ever
happened, even there, in the Borough of Bonhamtown

of Edison Township in the County of Middlesex,
where young ladies hike their skirts, drop

their green hair and skate the streets
with a backpack slung over one shoulder,

talking sweet smack until the big boys cower,
my name means nothing. Like most names,

mine was first handed down to a family
in another country whose penniless boys

had nowhere to go unless an American came
and sliced enough twenties from a wedge

to send their small, perfumed and newly bathed
crew of country-ass brown kids to rollick

with the light-skinned girls who worked
the edge of town. Then, for one night, the boys

could pay those dancers to call them whatever
they wanted. The name they gave me was

so empty you could put any landscape into it,
any country. I once put a lake inside it

and at the bottom of the water's murk,
the townspeople found a horse, just drowned.

When they cut the horse open, they found stones
the color of roses. Turns out, the stones

were worth something. So they gathered
kindling, chopped up the horse and cooked it

into a stew. The men who hauled the horse
from the water, not unlike some millions

of their time, were hungry. They dumped
the rose stones back into the lakehead

for someone else to one day harvest. And
they ate. Without a nickel to their names,

their stomachs stuffed with tough meat,
they stumbled drunk, out to the edge of town

and implored the girls to call them
John and Peter, Harry and Amoroso.

As for Montrose, I learned early on, if you follow it
far enough due north, this street changes its name.

When my mother married my father, as goes
the Western tradition, she changed her name

from Gelacio, which is Spanish, derived
from Gelasius, the Latin name of an African

pope, a Berber, they say. Look how far
a name can travel, crossing a sea borne

by a brown body whose old name
vanishes as one condition to rule

the Christian world, which he did,
according to some, with wicked orthodoxy.

I used to think the waters erased the names,
but who charts the waters charts the names

as well. The Spaniards trucked their God
from old Rome. And along with cannons

and garrotes, whetstones and coffers, Gelasius'
name was in the freight that came to a simple

village just inland from the Philippine Sea
where my mother would be born. In the end,

she lugged that name farther than Gelasius did,
from a coastal town in the tropics

to a drafty brickface with a ratty couch
and bad pipes. In Greek, her name means

full of laughter. Right now, the gleefullest
shouts bounding through the outerboroughs

belong, in part, to this kid and his two friends.
You could say, they make a sound that contains

my mother's name and I could track that
happy fracas from Bushwick to Kent and walk

far enough with them the long way toward
the Navy Yards after this block turns off, just

before they split toward their own route
home and I could stop and point out

the one-bedroom second-floor walkup
my father rented in 1964 for thirty-five dollars

a month. He paid in cash and the landlord said,
Father, let me show you how to live. My father

was a Father when my brother was born
and stopped being a Father when he became

a father to me—to be clear, he was a Catholic priest
until my mom got pregnant a second time.

The day my dad moved to Williamsburg, his landlord
drove him out to Chinatown and sat him at a dice game

where the puckish proprietor blew the rent
in an hour. The burly bouncers ushered the windbag

out by his elbow. My father followed. *That's
how to live, Nick.* My father's name is Nicholas,

but his family called him Charito, which is
the familiar diminutive of Rosario, or rosary,

the beads his mother held until her death,
counting the prescribed mysteries of their faith,

which has its rules, one of which is that
priests should not make love and women

should not make love to priests, but my mother
did, my father did, in secret, in the dark lots

and public parks of Chicago, until they escaped
that city's tsismis and my mother left, pregnant,

for Canada, my father landing in Brooklyn first,
in a half-bath flat on a street that trades its name

for a number before it ever reaches the river.
Brooklyn ends somewhere under water,

all the submerged wreckage joining this island
with the next. I wonder how many centuries

have left some American evidence in the name
of this thin-framed kid whose slick walk belies

the stiff green vines of the coming summer,
when his mother might call out her window for him

to set the table for dinner and some evenings
she might stay up real late waiting. I think

I know how a name can dangle mid-air as if
from a lamppost at dusk. How a mother's name

and a father's name can hang outside a window
or swing from a sad maple and no one will notice

among streetcorners first ordained in honor
of some fatcat or burning saint, but sometimes

we invent a name and its story for the hell of it,
for neither hell nor story is only ours

to remember. Here's proof: There once was a man
who put on a crown and made himself a king.

And his first order from the throne was to send
his governors out to issue new names

to each town. Among the hungry was a woman
who lived so long that, for generations, she

watched over the land upon which
thousands of wild horses stampeded, where

her whole tribe had built their homes, in which
they made love and broke each other's noses

and the horses snorted down from the hills'
crests every week of every decade of her life

and not once did she bear witness to a steed
mid-gallop flopped over so fast and so hard

it should open like a sudden rose, let alone
the gore of a hundred, of ten thousand. How

does a name become a field of beasts
become a field of flowers? How does any

such flood alter a field in secret and how
should an ancient field conceal the way

we say our original names? The woman,
those horses, the brutal floral funk that spells

a meadow long after the animals are gone?
I like to believe you can teach a child

to snip a blossom from a bloody thicket.
I like to believe you can learn to pinch

that simple bud, hold it to your lips, and
invoke the billion hidden names trilling within.

So when you join a dozen or one hundred
village elders, armed with small sickles,

having gathered from so many forgotten fields
some strange species of equine blossom,

you will place the flowers upon the dumb
governors' tables, which were first hewn,

hammered, and hand-lacquered by men
and women who never sat to eat — neither

simple meal nor feast. Listen:
                              our names

were taken. And in their place the bastards
shoved some other word like *laughter*

crafted with a Spanish hatchet or carved
like a joke into Roman stone. Every name

is a word embedded with a wish. Empire
is a word. Equinox is a word. In our time

you might see the sickles swarm in flowing
metallic droves to cut lost names from a field

of prickled stalks. You might see multitudes
come, not to watch the field but to reclaim it,

to slash a path all the way back to the tables
we first fashioned, to present our gruesome

harvest to our governors who—no surprise —
refuse to listen. To those ghastly murmurs

culled from the grisly pastures, that roll call
of the dying and nearly dead, they just

plug their ears with their fine royal wool.
                              Oh, Montrose,
four stops from the river and six from Union Square,

the woman who kept watch over the horses,
lived long enough to take her name back.

She whispered it into the field and the field
said the word over and over into its own deep dirt

and rock and billion-gnarl until the name
stayed for good, coded into its light at dusk.

There's a herd of bloody brutes that blossomed
before her eyes and here arrives your summer

child at my twenty-first century door,
late-March, the winter still stiffening our toes.

When I was a young man, I once had fifty singles
in my pocket. I thought I'd get to keep my name

from birth by writing it on dollar bills
or slipping those notes one by one across a bar

into the fingers of a woman working
the afternoon set among the turnpike

semis across the Hudson. It was enough
to pay for a couple drinks and an hour

to chat with a girl in pasties and a thong.
Like my father I thought I had nowhere

else to go. So in dirty cutoffs and flip flops
I followed desperate boys half way around

the world into the red light districts
where dozens of girls in riding boots or

stilettos scanned us for a balikbayan
(dipshit American? Even better.),

where you can choose a name
and lose your face in flashing neon.

But you have to remember the name
they gave you first. The one you came with.

My cousin, a younger man than me,
told me: if you manage to escape

any darkness (say a haunted grove
or thick wooded stretch patrolled by enemy

soldiers), right away, you have to turn
toward the dark. You have to shout

your own name back to make sure
your soul follows you into daylight

or at least into some dim street. You see,
that dark could belong to a precinct of captive

dancers, where, with your last fifty greenbacks,
you're supposed to order endless beers

and the girls will hug you all night and make you
think you're inventing a language to kiss them—

and another language to lie in bed
until dawn mostly alone—but those

women know the slick talk of every john
from Melbourne to Mississippi.

One morning I tipped the madame and flagged
a taxi bloodshot. A light rain spat down.

Back at my uncle's house, I thought
it might be beautiful to shut the blinds

and listen to the tapping as it steadied,
heavy on the corrugated roofs

through night into the next morning,
the slow gathering of a trillion hammers

spiking the metal overhead, not one
wind in the streets. The sewer line out

near the national highway and the six-block
gash in the blacktop under repair filled quick

with rain, chasing the mice into every bedroom.
I might not get to the body count the typhoon

left behind, how it circled back, zig-zagged
for a second rip-and-run across the island.

Let's just say they baptize natural disasters
as if we could call them closer or coax them back

to where they come from: Katrina, Sandy, Ondoy.
During that last storm, it took two weeks

before the worst of the waters receded,
before they found three men rotting in a tree.

No one had looked up. But for the sweet
reek wafting down, no one would have seen them

drowning in the sky. It's what happens when
a storm keeps stirring a river and a river

keeps taking, flushing shanties down main roads
towing more than 3,000 bodies below.

Even the governor's snorting horses flopped
onto their sides, the tonnage whisked off

tumbling in the current and I'll save the story
of the yard-hand who hid a sack of stolen

stones and their scarlet glow, how he shoved them
over the course of weeks before the storm

into the mouth of his master's favorite parade horse
suffering from colic. The floods

left the boy and took the horse.
                                        Metropolis,
do you hear me? Young man? I don't want

anything. I want this. I want to say
the names we've been given aloud. The ones

they took away. I want to shout out the names
of those who named us. I want to go back

far enough that all of memory gets cloudy
and we have to—as our grandfathers

and grandmothers have done for more
than four hundred years—make it up,

even if all we got now is the whiff of a river
swelling, the half-truths and full lies inscribed

in books packed in a middle-school satchel
on a cool day in Brooklyn. I live

in a country where the legends
are illegible or torn off. I wake up

on a block where I can watch from a distance
100,000 billboards alter the nighttime

sky, the kind of lights that could change
the bodies of horses in a field before

your very eyes, dashing down a meadow,
the thorns burst from their rumps

and mouths and undersides blooming bloody.
What do I know anyway... I'm the one

who believes we have ancient names
like dawnlight flashing into the dreams

of murderers and sunken into the hillsides
of countries whose shanties and projects

are named for moguls and saints, though
children drown here, just like they do

everywhere: Manila, New Orleans,
Brooklyn. There's not a name that fits.

You could flood an avenue with storm-
water or roses or the horses could suddenly

split down their bellies mid-stampede.
Your name could curse a city. And it would be

a calamity. It would be spring.

ACKNOWLEDGMENTS

Thanks to following journals and sites, which originally published poems in this collection, sometimes in previous versions: *Alaska Quarterly Review, Ampersand Review, Apogee, At Length, The Collagist, Exit 7, Four Way Review, Gulf Coast, Mead, New England Review, Poetry,* Poets.org, *Southern Illinois Review, Tin House, Union Station Magazine, Waxwing*

"You Cannot Go to the God You Love with Your Two Legs" was reprinted in *Best American Poetry.*

"A Scavenger's Ode to the Turntable (Or a Note To Thomas Alva Edison)" is for Junji, Phil, and Jo Malamug
"At the Tribunals" is for Terence Calulo
"Uptown Ode That Ends On an Ode to the Machete" is for Willie (with big up to Orlando and G-Bo)
"Ode to Not Having Enough Kids to Play a Game of Baseball" is for my brothers, Anthony and Mark
"Wish" is for Remi and Milo
"Despedida: Quezon City" is for all my friends and family in the Metro Manila area, especially the Xavierville/QC crew, much love.

Completion of the writing of this book was supported by a fellowship from the U.S. State Department's Fulbright program and Rutgers University's Faculty Research Grant program. I'm grateful to both for the time and resources made available to me.

Many thanks are due to people who have supported me and my work (and play): my family, especially Anthony, Mark, Heidi, Joyce, Remi, Milo, Christine, Tony Dozier, Kalesi, my dad, Tita Thelma, the whole Narciso clan, the whole Gelacio clan, especially Joey Gelacio, Oca Gelacio, Junrex Pablo and Boy Duldulao, also Rose McGrane, Emy Cella, Ed Narciso, James Narciso, Jay Narciso, their families, my Auntie Uding (Rest in peace), the Triunfante-Lucas-Invencion Chicago crew (much love to you for feeding me and giving me a place to stay), the good people of Balacad for the history that goes back before it was written down though it's coded in our blood, the good people of Sikatuna and Quezon City, Tita Cion, Uncle Oscar Inocentes, the Llanes and Rosal clans, the Portugal and Piano families, Krip Yuson, Jimmy Abad, Rock Drilon, Joel Toledo, Pancho Villanueva, Sasha Martinez, Drea Teran, Rafael San Diego, Mikael de Lara Co, Maggie Costello, Daryll Delgado, William Ragamat, Jiggs Baarde, Mitzi Borromeo, Maria Isabel Garcia, OK Baguio I holler at you too, Frank Cimatu, my whole Jersey folks (I know crew love changes over time, but you're always in my heart, for real for real), for bringing me to this work and reminding me what matters: Paul Genega, the late John Carey, the late Marty Kellman, colleagues former and current, to every-one who reads and teaches my work, to those who wrestle with and argue against it, to those who pass it on in the air and in the electric lake and on the page, A. Van Jordan, Tyehimba Jess, Samantha Thornhill, Elana Bell, Suzanne Gardinier, Randall Horton, Sarah Gambito, Joseph Legaspi, Oliver de la Paz, Vikas Menon, Jennifer Chang, Aimee Nezhukumtathil, my most valuable first readers, without whom this book just wouldn't happen not one bit not at all: Ross Gay, Aracelis Girmay, Roger Bonair-Agard, Curtis C-Boogie Bauer, Steve Scafidi, my most dearest Karissa Chen—who has kept me sane and shared good meals and so much laughter and has believed in my work and challenged me to be a better man, a bet-ter thinker, a better heart—Lynne Procope, John Murillo, Nicole Sealey, Eileen Tabios, Ron Villanueva, Jason Koo, Tiphanie Yanique, Aisha Moon, Rachel Eliza Griffiths, Syreeta McFadden, Tish Vallés, Kevin Coval, Shara McCallum, Simone White, Martín Espada, Jeff Kass, Angel Nafis, Jon Pineda, Evelina Galang, Eugene Gloria, Luis Francia, Lara Stapleton, Bino Realuyo, Gina Apostol, Eric Gamalinda, Willie Perdomo, Marty McConnell, Gerald Stern, Alicia Ostriker, Jean Valentine, Ira Sadoff, Paul Lisicky, Gabrielle Calvocoressi, Vijay Seshadri, Thomas Lux, Marie Howe, Quincy Troupe, Ellen Dore Watson, Anne Marie Macari, Judith Vollmer, Michael Waters, Mihaela Moscaliuc, Bob Holman, Latasha Nevada Diggs, Matthew Olzmann, Nandi Comer, Eliel Lucero, Aiza Galdo, Junot Díaz, Jessica Hagedorn, Terrance Hayes, David Wright, Idoia Elola, Rich Villar, Fish Vargas, Emily and Geoff Kagan-Trenchard, Christine Balance, Joseph Ponce, Krista Franklin, Ruth Ellen Kocher, Phil Malamug, Junji Malamug, Monica Malamug, Jojo Malamug, the Malamug clan, Uncle Ernie (RIP) and Tita Cands and my cousin Joy, Joan

Larkin, Chris White, Martha Labare, Sekou Sundiata (RIP), Alexandra Soiseth, Kyes Stevens, PAEF staff, Fulbright/IIE. Special thanks to my editor and friend Gabriel Fried for more than a decade of collaboration, and much gratitude to Michael Braziller and Karen Braziller. I would also like to my family in Oahu and the Big Island; you are all in my heart and in these pages, so much affection to you. I couldn't have written this book without the kindness, love, and stories of Uncle Charlie and Auntie Celia and the rest of my extended family in Laoag, Ilocos Norte. Thank you all.